Toddler meals

To my children, Nicholas, Lara and Scarlett

Toddler meals

Nutritious recipes for your child to enjoy with the family

annabel karmel

1 3 5 7 9 10 8 6 4 2

Text copyright © Annabel Karmel 2006, 2007, 2009, 2010, 2011, 2013
Photographs copyright © Dave King 2006, 2009, 2010, 2011, 2013,
except pages 22 and 35 Daniel Pangbourne 2001
and pages 16, 21, 66, 84 and 91 Ebury Press 2007
This edition copyright © Eddison Sadd Editions 2013

The Random House Group Limited Reg. No. 954009

A CIP catalogue record for this book is available from the British Library

ISBN: 978-009-195579-3

Printed in Hong Kong

Eddison•Sadd Editions

CREATIVE DIRECTOR Nick Eddison   INDEXER Dorothy Frame
SENIOR EDITOR Katie Golsby   DESIGNER Brazzle Atkins
PROOFREADER Nikky Twyman   ILLUSTRATIONS Nadine Wikenden
PRODUCTION Sarah Rooney
COVER PHOTOGRAPHY Dave King

Notes on the text:
· For fan-assisted ovens, reduce the temperature by 20°C.
· All black pepper is freshly ground.

Contents

Introduction

Once babies enter the toddler years, things often change quite a bit in the eating department. In an ideal world, our children would happily eat a varied, healthy diet giving them all the nutrients and vitamins they need during this period of growth. However, I find that, at this stage, babies want to assert their independence, and getting them to eat the nutritious fare that's put in front of them may be a trial.

From the age of one year, your toddler will be keen to feed herself, her fingers often being the eating tools of choice. It's a good idea to let her experiment with her fingers and toddler cutlery; it won't come naturally, so needs a little practice. This may mean you have to brace yourself for a bit of mess. If your toddler struggles to get the hang of using a spoon to begin with, try giving soft finger foods.

Finger foods

Finger foods are great for toddlers: you can give raw vegetable sticks, breads and meats, but you must still be careful about foods such as whole nuts, olives and any other hard foods that could be swallowed. Toddlers love to put anything and everything in their mouths, and it would be very easy for them to choke on such foods.

Snacks

This stage of development involves a lot of high-energy activity, so it's a good idea to give your little one three meals a day. Snacks in between are a good idea if they are at regular times and aren't given too often or just before meals. Stick to healthy foods and don't let your child graze throughout the day. We are a nation of fussy eaters, and continuously giving children snacks and not allowing them to get hungry is part of the problem.

Good snacks include fruit or vegetable slices, baby rice cakes, dried fruit, bread sticks and cheese. It's a good idea to have some of these ready in the fridge, so you have something to hand when you're faced with a hungry toddler. If you cut up a few carrots and put them in cold water in an airtight container, they will last for several days. Enjoying regular healthy snacks is a good habit to get your child into and can instil a love of healthy food early on.

That isn't to say that chocolate and biscuits should be banned; I believe that forbidding something can make more tempting. But if your child isn't used to having regular sugary snacks, she isn't likely to miss them if they aren't there. Plus, if you don't have these things in the house as standard, they become much more of a treat – it also stops *you* from eating them! Children pick up habits from their parents, so if they see you feasting on chocolate, they will want some too.

What foods to give

To a great extent, your toddler can eat what you eat. It's important to get children eating 'grown-up food' as early as possible; as children tend to get fussier as they get older, it's easier to make this transition sooner rather than later. It also saves on you having to cook different dishes. Obviously, levels of salt and spice need to be reduced.

Many toddlers like much more interesting flavours than you might think: mildly spicy food and meals like stir-fries, egg fried rice (*see page 41*) and chicken satay (*see page 51*) are often very popular. Putting food on skewers (watch out for sharp ends) or using chopsticks can be good fun and are great ways to get the whole family involved in mealtimes.

Nutritional needs

Children under the age of five need more dietary fat than adults, so avoid giving low-fat varieties of foods such as milk, yoghurt and cheese. High-fibre foods are also inappropriate, as they can hinder the absorption of vitamins and minerals.

If you're bringing your child up as a vegetarian, or she won't eat meat, make sure her diet includes sources of protein such as eggs, cheese and pulses. As she isn't eating red meat, you will also need to ensure that she's getting enough iron from other sources, such as lentils or leafy green vegetables. These need to be accompanied by a good source of vitamin C, in order for the iron to be well absorbed.

Start the day well

It's essential to start the day with a nutritious breakfast, to keep us energized until lunchtime. Wholegrain cereals like porridge and granola release sugars slowly, avoiding the highs and lows of refined cereals, and are ideal for children. Unfortunately, many of the cereals designed for children contain more than 30 per cent sugar. Read the labels carefully, and check that the cereal contains less than 10 g ($\frac{1}{4}$ oz) of sugar per 100 g ($3\frac{1}{2}$ oz). It's a good idea for your child to have a glass of orange juice with breakfast, as this will help him to absorb the iron from the cereal.

Eggs, such as scrambled eggs and boiled eggs with soldiers, also make a great breakfast. See pages 13 and 14 for some recipe ideas to try.

Fussy eaters

In a recent survey, the Euro Toddler Nutrition Index showed that British toddlers were the most likely in Europe to refuse foods. Around 90 per cent of children go through at least one lengthy stage of fussy eating, and it can be unbelievably frustrating. However, I believe that the key is not letting your child see how stressed it makes you feel. Refusing food will lose its appeal if you don't react or offer a sugary treat as a bribe. Ignore any bad behaviour and be incredibly enthusiastic when your toddler does try something new, even if it's a tiny amount.

Don't worry about letting your fussy child starve; when she is hungry, she will eat. Toddlers can survive on only a little food, and their tastes can change dramatically from one day to the next – one day's favourite food could be completely refused the following day. Keep an eye on how much your child drinks, as this can affect hunger. Drinking lots of juice or having too many snacks in between meals could mean she isn't interested in food at mealtimes.

Small and appealing

It's a good idea to give small portions at this stage. Toddlers can be overwhelmed when faced by a large amount of food, particularly if they tend to be fussy. Making the meal look appealing can also make a real difference to whether it gets eaten or not. Make meals interesting and fun. There are so many great ways to capture a child's interest in food, even if it does involve having a laugh over a face you've made out of peas.

Recipe information

Each recipe is accompanied by helpful information on preparation and cooking times, how many portions the recipe makes and whether it's suitable for freezing. Preparation times and portion quantities should be used as a guide only, as these will vary.

On pages 92–3, you will find a meal planner to help you to stay organized. This is intended to be used for guidance; you can, of course, use different recipes if you wish.

This book is a collection of some of my favourite meals for toddlers. However, they're not *just* for toddlers; they're designed to appeal to the whole family, so tuck in and enjoy!

Breakfast

Perfect scrambled eggs

Crack the eggs into a bowl and add the milk. Whisk until well combined. Melt the butter in a pan. When it starts to sizzle, pour in the egg mixture. Immediately reduce the heat to Medium or Low. Sprinkle with a little salt and pepper to taste. Stir gently. When the egg looks wet but is no longer liquid, remove from the heat. Stir in any extras, such as those listed here.

✎ 3 MINUTES

▭ 5 MINUTES

◷ 2 PORTIONS

✳ NOT SUITABLE FOR FREEZING

2 eggs
2 tablespoons milk
a generous knob of butter
salt and pepper

Optional extras
fresh chives or other herbs
spring onion, chopped
cheese, grated
ham, diced
tomatoes, chopped

Eggs provide an excellent source of protein, zinc and vitamins A, D, E and B12. Although eggs are high in cholesterol, this has very little effect compared to things like obesity and smoking, and isn't anything to worry about.

Soft-boiled egg with Italian soldiers

 5 MINUTES

 4 MINUTES

1 PORTION

NOT SUITABLE FOR FREEZING

1 medium egg
2 slices prosciutto or
   Parma ham, cut in half
   lengthways
2 breadsticks, broken in half

Bring a large saucepan of water to the boil, then reduce to a brisk simmer. Using a large spoon, gently lower in the egg and cook for 4 minutes (for a runny yolk and a set white).

Meanwhile, wrap one of the pieces of prosciutto around one of the breadstick halves, starting at the broken end, and wrap twisting downwards and slightly overlapping, so that around two-thirds of the breadstick is covered in ham. Press the ham firmly on itself to seal. Repeat so that you have four 'Italian soldiers'.

Transfer the egg to an egg cup and cut off the top. Dip the Italian soldiers in the egg yolk and enjoy!

Do not give lightly cooked eggs to babies under the age of one.

Annabel's granola

Lightly oil a baking sheet. Preheat the oven to 150°C/300°F/Gas 2.

Put the oats, pecans, coconut, salt and sugar into a large bowl and mix with a wooden spoon.

Whisk the oil and maple syrup together in a jug or small bowl. Pour over the oats and mix well.

Spread out the mixture on the prepared baking sheet and bake in the centre of the oven for 40–45 minutes, stirring every 10 minutes. Transfer to a bowl, stir in the raisins and leave to cool.

✐ 5 MINUTES

▦ 45 MINUTES (PLUS COOLING)

◉ 6–8 PORTIONS

❋ NOT SUITABLE FOR FREEZING

175 g (6 oz) rolled oats
70 g (2½ oz) pecans, coarsely chopped
20 g (¾ oz) shredded or desiccated coconut
¼ teaspoon salt
60 g (2 oz) soft brown sugar
2 tablespoons sunflower oil
4 tablespoons maple syrup
50 g (2 oz) raisins

This delicious granola is very versatile. Serve it for breakfast with milk or layered with yoghurt, honey and fruit, or on its own as a snack. If your child is allergic to nuts – or just dislikes them – you could use pumpkin seeds instead, or double the quantity of raisins.

Toasted crumpets with banana and peanut butter

/ 1 MINUTE

⊞ 5 MINUTES

◷ 1 PORTION

✳ NOT SUITABLE FOR FREEZING

2 crumpets
2 tablespoons peanut butter
a little honey
1 small banana, sliced

Preheat the grill and toast the crumpets on both sides. Remove them and spread one side with peanut butter. Drizzle over the honey and arrange the banana on top. Place under the grill for another couple of minutes.

Ham and cheese muffins

Preheat the grill to High. Toast the muffins in a toaster. Mix the cream cheese and Cheddar together, then spread over the toasted muffins. Top with the ham and tomato. Grill for 4–5 minutes, until melted and lightly golden.

🔪 3 MINUTES

🖻 7–8 MINUTES

🕓 2 PORTIONS

❄ NOT SUITABLE FOR FREEZING

2 English muffins, sliced
in half
50 g (2 oz) cream cheese
50 g (2 oz) mature Cheddar
cheese, grated
2 slices of ham, chopped
1 tomato, washed and sliced

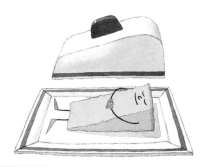

Cheese is a perfect food for children. It provides an excellent source of protein and calcium, which are both important for strong bones and good teeth.

Berry burst

 5 MINUTES

 MAKES 1 GLASS

❋ NOT SUITABLE FOR FREEZING

85 g (3 oz) fresh or frozen
  summer berries
1 small banana, peeled and
  cut into chunks
3 tablespoons strawberry
  yoghurt
2 teaspoons clear honey
4 tablespoons milk

If you're using frozen fruits, leave them to defrost for about 20 minutes.

Put the berries, banana, yoghurt and honey into a blender and whiz for 1–2 minutes, until smooth. Add the milk and whiz again until frothy. Pour into a glass to serve.

Most children love summer fruits, but if they find the seeds off-putting, pass the blended smoothie through a sieve before serving.

Vegetables

Vegetable pasta

Cook the pasta following the packet instructions. Add the broccoli 3 minutes before the end of the cooking time, then drain.

Heat the oil in a frying pan. Add the leek and fry for 3 minutes, then add the squash and fry for another 3 minutes, until just cooked. Add the mushrooms, then the stock, soy sauce, lemon juice and garlic purée. Stir in the pasta and crème fraîche, then add the Parmesan. Toss together over the heat and season well.

Pasta is a great energy food, packed full of carbohydrates, which are broken down to supply all the cells in our bodies with fuel.

✎ 10 MINUTES

▦ 10 MINUTES

◷ 4 PORTIONS

✳ SUITABLE FOR FREEZING

225 g (8 oz) fusilli pasta
125 g (4½ oz) broccoli florets, washed
2 tablespoons sunflower oil
150 g (5 oz) leek, washed, peeled and sliced
100 g (3½ oz) butternut squash, peeled, deseeded and chopped
75 g (3 oz) mushrooms, washed and sliced
200 ml (7 fl oz) chicken or vegetable stock
2 tablespoons soy sauce (preferably from a sachet)
1 teaspoon lemon juice
1 teaspoon garlic purée
100 g (3½ oz) crème fraîche
50 g (2 oz) Parmesan cheese, grated
salt and pepper

Tortilla Pizza Margherita

⟋ 5 MINUTES

▦ 8–9 MINUTES

🍽 1 PORTION

✳ NOT SUITABLE FOR FREEZING

1 wheat tortilla wrap
2½ tablespoons tomato
  sauce (*see box, right*)
30 g (1 oz) Cheddar or
  mozzarella cheese, grated

Toppings
2–3 black olives, stoned and
  cut into rings
1 cherry tomato, cut into rings
2 cubes tinned pineapple,
  drained and diced
1 tablespoon diced red pepper
1 tablespoon drained tinned
  sweetcorn
1 spring onion, sliced
2 mushrooms, sliced and
  sautéed in a little oil
3–4 very thin courgette slices,
  brushed with a little oil
1 tablespoon grated
  Parmesan
2 sunblush tomatoes,
  chopped

Preheat the oven to 200°C/400°F/Gas 6. Put the tortilla wrap on a baking sheet and spread over the tomato sauce. Sprinkle over the cheese. Add any toppings that your child may like (see the suggestions below left). Bake for 8–9 minutes, until the cheese has melted and the base is crisp. Cut into triangles and allow to cool slightly before serving.

Wheat tortilla wraps are perfect for small children who find the slim base easier to eat than a normal pizza base. Sometimes the air bubbles in the wrap puff up a bit as the pizza bakes, but they deflate as soon as they come out of the oven, so don't panic!

For the tomato sauce, use your favourite recipe or a shop-bought variety.

I would suggest you don't use more than two toppings per pizza.

Puff-pastry pizzas

Preheat the oven to 200°C/400°F/Gas 6. Roll out the pastry to form a 20 x 25 cm (8 x 10 in) rectangle. Divide the pastry into quarters and place on a baking sheet. Prick the pizza bases with a fork.

Mix the cream cheese and pesto together and spread over the pizza bases. Arrange the tomato slices on top, then the basil, and sprinkle with the cheese. Bake for 15–20 minutes, until puffed up and golden brown.

/ 10 MINUTES

▢ 15–20 MINUTES

◔ 4 SMALL PIZZAS

✳ SUITABLE FOR FREEZING

250 g (9 oz) puff pastry
   (shop-bought is fine)
1 tablespoon cream cheese
1 tablespoon pesto
4 tomatoes, washed and
   sliced
a few fresh basil leaves,
   chopped
100 g (3½ oz) mature
   Cheddar cheese, grated

Cheese is particularly beneficial at the end of a meal, as it raises the calcium concentration in plaque. Protein from cheese is also absorbed onto the enamel surface of the teeth and physically slows down tooth decay.

Carrot and pea risotto

🗲 10 MINUTES

⬜ 20 MINUTES

🍳 4–6 PORTIONS

❄ SUITABLE FOR FREEZING

1 tablespoon olive oil
1 onion (about 140 g/5 oz),
    peeled and chopped
1 carrot (about 100 g/3½ oz),
    peeled and chopped
1 courgette (about 200 g/
    7 oz), washed, topped and
    tailed, and chopped
2 garlic cloves, crushed
125 g (4½ oz) risotto rice
450 ml (¾ pint) chicken
    stock
50 g (2 oz) frozen peas
50 g (2 oz) Parmesan cheese,
    grated
2 tablespoons chopped basil
juice of half a lemon

Preheat the oven to 170°C/325°F/Gas 3. Heat the olive oil in an ovenproof saucepan or casserole dish. Add the onion, carrot and courgette, and fry for 2 minutes. Add the garlic and rice, then blend in the stock. Bring to the boil, cover and transfer to the oven for 10 minutes. Add the peas and return to the oven for 5 minutes, until the rice is just cooked. Finally, stir in the Parmesan, basil and lemon.

Carrots do improve night vision. They are a great source of betacarotene, which is formed in the body into vitamin A – one of the first symptoms of vitamin A deficiency is night blindness.

Crudités and dips

To make any of these dips, mix all the ingredients together and transfer to a ramekin. For the sweet chilli and cream-cheese dip, you could spoon the chilli sauce over the cream cheese and chives if you prefer.

⊛ NOT SUITABLE FOR FREEZING

Serve with cucumber, carrot, sweet pepper sticks and cherry tomatoes for dipping, or try some more unusual vegetables, such as sugar snap peas. Pitta bread and breadsticks also work well.

Thousand island dip
2 tablespoons Greek yoghurt
2 tablespoons mayonnaise
2 teaspoons tomato ketchup
½ teaspoon lemon juice
1–2 drops Worcestershire sauce

Mango and cream-cheese dip
4 tablespoons cream cheese
3 tablespoons natural yoghurt
1½ tablespoons mango chutney
1 tablespoon lemon juice
a pinch of curry powder
salt and pepper, to taste

Sweet chilli and cream-cheese dip
100 g (3½ oz) cream cheese
1 teaspoon chopped chives
1 teaspoon sweet chilli sauce

Ranch dip
3 tablespoons sour cream
2 tablespoons mayonnaise
1 teaspoon lime juice (optional)
1 teaspoon chopped coriander
1 teaspoon chopped chives
salt and pepper, to taste

Carrot and sweetcorn fritters

⏱ 10 MINUTES

🔲 10 MINUTES

🍳 10 FRITTERS

❄ SUITABLE FOR FREEZING

50 g (2 oz) self-raising flour
1 egg
1 tablespoon milk
1 medium carrot (100 g/
  3½ oz), peeled and grated
50 g (2 oz) courgette,
  washed, topped and
  tailed, and grated
½ medium red onion (about
  75 g/3 oz), peeled and
  finely chopped
2 tablespoons drained
  tinned sweetcorn
2 tablespoons chopped basil
1 tablespoon sweet chilli
  sauce
50 g (2 oz) Cheddar cheese,
  grated
salt and pepper
a little oil for frying

Put the flour, egg and milk into a bowl. Mix together, then add all the remaining ingredients except for the oil.

Heat the oil in a frying pan, drop in tablespoonfuls of the mixture, and fry for 2–3 minutes on each side.

Unlike many vegetables, carrots are most nutritious when cooked. Cooking breaks open the plant cells, so antioxidants and other plant chemicals can be absorbed more easily.

Baby spinach and tomato gnocchi

/ 7 MINUTES

▢ 20 MINUTES

◷ 4 PORTIONS

❄ SUITABLE FOR FREEZING

400 g (14 oz) gnocchi
50 g (2 oz) baby spinach
1 tablespoon olive oil
1 onion, peeled and chopped
1 garlic clove, crushed
500 g (1 lb 2 oz) passata
1 tablespoon sun-dried
   tomato paste
½ teaspoon dried oregano
2 teaspoons sugar
3 tablespoons double cream
salt and pepper
50 g (2 oz) mozzarella
   cheese, diced
30 g (1 oz) Parmesan cheese,
   grated

Cook the gnocchi according to the packet instructions, adding the spinach for the last 30 seconds of the cooking time. Drain.

Heat the oil in a saucepan. Add the onion and garlic and fry for 5 minutes, until softened. Add the passata, tomato paste, oregano and sugar, and simmer for 5 minutes. Then stir in the cream. Tip the gnocchi and spinach into the sauce, then season.

Preheat the grill to High. Spoon the mixture into a shallow heatproof dish, and top with the mozzarella and Parmesan. Place under the grill for 5 minutes.

Spinach is a good source of betacarotene and vitamin C; don't overcook it, or you will destroy a lot of its content. Despite popular opinion – and Popeye – it's not a particularly good source of iron.

Fish

Mini fish pies

✏ 3 MINUTES

▦ 15–20 MINUTES

◷ 4 PORTIONS

❉ SUITABLE FOR FREEZING

400 g (14 oz) potatoes,
   peeled and cut into chunks
2 medium carrots (150 g/
   5 oz), peeled and chopped
25 g (1 oz) butter, plus extra
   for mashing
1 medium onion (about
   140 g/5 oz), peeled and
   chopped
25 g (1 oz) plain flour
300 ml (½ pint) milk, plus 2
   tablespoons for mashing
2 teaspoons lemon juice
2 teaspoons chopped dill
30 g (1 oz) Parmesan cheese,
   grated
300 g (11 oz) cod fillet, or 150 g
   (5 oz) each of cod and
   salmon fillet, skinned and
   cubed
salt and pepper

Preheat the oven to 200°C/400°F/Gas 6. Put the potatoes and carrots into a large saucepan. Cover with cold water, bring to the boil and simmer for 15 minutes, until tender.

Meanwhile, melt the butter in a saucepan. Add the onion and sauté until lightly golden. Add the flour and stir over the heat. Blend in the milk and bring to the boil, stirring until thickened. Remove from the heat and add the lemon juice, dill and Parmesan. Add the fish and season to taste. Spoon into 4 ramekins.

Drain the potatoes and carrots and mash. Stir in a knob of butter and the remaining milk. Spoon on top of the ramekins and fluff up the surfaces with a fork. Bake for 15 minutes, until bubbling.

Salmon provides a good source of essential fats that support brain function and the immune system. These fats are believed to help children who suffer from dyslexia or dyspraxia.

Chinese-style fish fillets

First, make the sauce. Mix together the stock, soy sauce, sesame oil, sugar, cider vinegar and cornflour. Pour into a saucepan, bring to the boil and then simmer, stirring, for 2–3 minutes, until thickened and smooth. Stir in the spring onion.

Heat 1 tablespoon of the vegetable oil in a pan, and sauté the courgette and red pepper for 4 minutes.

Season the flour and dip the fish in it so it is lightly coated. Heat the remaining oil in a frying pan, then sauté the fish for about 3 minutes on each side, until cooked through.

Add the vegetables, pour over the sauce and cook for 2 minutes.

✎ 5 MINUTES

⬛ 20 MINUTES

🍽 2 PORTIONS

❄ SUITABLE FOR FREEZING

3 tablespoons vegetable oil
1 small courgette (100 g/ 3½ oz), washed, topped and tailed, and cut into strips
½ red pepper (50 g/2 oz), washed, deseeded and cut into strips
salt and pepper
plain flour, to coat
350 g (12 oz) plaice or sole fillets, skinned and cut into 6.5 cm (2½ in) strips

Sauce
250 ml (8 fl oz) chicken or fish stock
10 ml (½ fl oz) soy sauce
1 teaspoon sesame oil
1 tablespoon sugar
1 teaspoon cider vinegar
1 tablespoon cornflour
1 spring onion, washed and finely sliced

Cod in cheesy sauce

✎ 10 MINUTES

▭ 20 MINUTES

🕒 3–4 PORTIONS

❄ SUITABLE FOR FREEZING

300 g (11 oz) potatoes,
 peeled and cut into chunks
25 g (1 oz) butter
1 medium onion (about
 140 g/5 oz), peeled and
 finely chopped
2 level tablespoons plain
 flour
2 teaspoons rice wine
 vinegar
300 ml (½ pint) milk
25 g (1 oz) Parmesan cheese,
 grated
250 g (9 oz) cod fillet,
 skinned and cut into 3 cm
 (1¼ in) cubes
2 tablespoons chopped
 chives
2 tablespoons milk
15 g (½ oz) butter

Put the potatoes into a large saucepan, cover
with boiling water and cook for about 20 minutes,
until tender.

Meanwhile, melt the butter in a saucepan.
Add the onion and simmer for 5 minutes, until
soft. Add the flour, then the rice wine vinegar.
Blend in the milk. Bring to the boil, stirring until
thickened. Add the Parmesan, then the cod.
Simmer gently for 3–4 minutes, until the fish is
cooked. Add the chives.

Drain the potatoes and mash together with
the milk and butter.

*White fish such as cod is an excellent source of
low-fat protein and contains selenium, calcium
and magnesium. Eating fish helps fight free
radicals and also boosts the immune system.*

Sticky salmon

3 MINUTES, PLUS 1 HOUR
FOR MARINATING

10 MINUTES

4 PORTIONS

NOT SUITABLE FOR FREEZING

2 salmon fillets (about 200 g/
7 oz), skinned and cut into
4 cm (1½ in) cubes

Marinade
1½ tablespoons soy sauce
2 tablespoons tomato
   ketchup
1 tablespoon white wine
   vinegar
½ teaspoon sweet chilli sauce
1½ tablespoons dark brown
   sugar

Place all the ingredients for the marinade in a
small saucepan and stir over a gentle heat until
the sugar has dissolved. Remove from the heat,
pour into a medium-size bowl and leave to cool.
Add the salmon cubes and coat them in the
sauce. Leave to marinate for at least 1 hour.

Preheat the grill to High and line a baking
sheet with aluminium foil. Place in the salmon,
pour over the marinade and grill for about
5 minutes, turning halfway through and basting
occasionally until cooked. Remove the salmon
from the tin and serve with Easy Chinese Fried
Rice (*see right*).

Easy Chinese fried rice

Cook the rice following the packet instructions, adding the carrot to the pan. Then, 4 minutes before the end of the cooking time, add the peas.

Meanwhile, heat the oil in a frying pan or wok, beat the egg with a little salt, and pour into the pan, tilting it so that the egg coats the base. Cook until it sets as a thin omelette. Remove from the pan, roll up to form a sausage shape and cut into thin strips.

Melt the butter in the wok and sauté the onion for 2 minutes. Add the rice, carrot and peas, the soy sauce and a little freshly ground black pepper. Stir-fry the rice for about 2 minutes, then stir in the strips of egg and the spring onion and heat through.

Serve with Sticky Salmon (*see left*).

 6 MINUTES

 12 MINUTES

4 PORTIONS

NOT SUITABLE FOR FREEZING

200 g (7 oz) basmati rice
1 small carrot (65 g/2½ oz), peeled and finely chopped
75 g (3 oz) frozen peas
1 teaspoon vegetable oil
1 egg, lightly beaten
a pinch of salt
25 g (1 oz) butter
1 small onion (65 g/2½ oz), peeled and finely chopped
2 tablespoons soy sauce
freshly ground black pepper
1 spring onion, washed and finely sliced

Teriyaki salmon

- 🔪 5 MINUTES
- ▢ 8 MINUTES
- 🕐 6 SKEWERS
- ✴ NOT SUITABLE FOR FREEZING

1 tablespoon sesame seeds
200 g (7 oz) skinless salmon
  fillet, cut into 1 cm (⅓ in)
  cubes
¼ teaspoon grated fresh
  root ginger
1½ teaspoons dark soy sauce
1 tablespoon clear honey
6 wooden skewers, soaked
  in water for 30 minutes

First, line a baking sheet with aluminium foil.

Toast the sesame seeds in a small frying pan over a medium heat for 2–3 minutes, stirring two or three times. Spread them out on a plate and allow to cool.

Thread 3 or 4 cubes of salmon onto each skewer and place the skewers on the prepared baking sheet.

Preheat the grill to High. To make the teriyaki sauce, put the ginger, soy sauce and honey into a bowl and mix together. Brush some of the sauce onto the salmon and grill for 2 minutes, as close to the heat as possible. Brush more teriyaki sauce onto the salmon and grill for another 2 minutes. Turn the skewers over, and repeat the brushing and grilling process.

Cool the skewers slightly and sprinkle with the toasted sesame seeds. For smaller children, it may be a good idea to remove the skewers before serving.

Posh fish fingers

Pat the fish dry with paper towels and cut into strips the size of a little finger (you should have about 16 strips). Spread out the flour on a large plate. Combine the breadcrumbs, Parmesan and lemon zest on another large plate and season with a good pinch of paprika and some seasoning. Crack the egg into a small bowl and beat well with a pinch of salt.

Toss the fish in the flour and shake off any excess, then dip in the egg and, finally, roll in the crumb mixture.

Heat the oil in a large frying pan or wok, over a medium heat, and fry the fish goujons for 1½–2 minutes on each side, until golden and cooked through. Drain on kitchen paper and allow to cool slightly before serving.

⟋ 15 MINUTES

▭ 10 MINUTES

◔ 4 PORTIONS

✳ SUITABLE FOR FREEZING (UNCOOKED)

170 g (6 oz) skinless lemon sole fillets (or similar, like plaice, flounder or tilapia)
2 tablespoons plain flour
55 g (2 oz) Panko breadcrumbs or dried breadcrumbs
30 g (1 oz) Parmesan cheese, grated
½ teaspoon finely grated lemon zest
paprika, to taste
salt and pepper
1 egg
4–5 tablespoons sunflower oil, for frying

Japanese Panko breadcrumbs are extremely light and crispy and make a good coating for fish. They are available in Asian markets and stores, as well as some large supermarkets.

To freeze, put the uncooked goujons on a baking sheet lined with clingfilm. Freeze for 2–3 hours, until solid, then transfer to freezer bags. Cook from frozen, adding 30 seconds to the cooking time.

Chicken

Chicken marinades

Mix together all the ingredients for your chosen marinade. Transfer to a resealable bag or a bowl with the chicken, and marinate in the fridge for at least 1 hour. Season the chicken before cooking, but don't add the seasoning to the marinade.

When you are ready to cook, preheat the grill to High and thread the chicken onto the skewers. Line a baking sheet with aluminium foil and grill the chicken for 3–4 minutes on each side. Alternatively, you can cook them on a griddle.

🖉 5–10 MINUTES, PLUS 1 HOUR FOR MARINATING

⬜ 8–10 MINUTES

⏰ 2–4 PORTIONS

❄ SUITABLE FOR FREEZING

For each marinade
110 g (4 oz) chicken mini fillets, or boneless skinless chicken breast, cut into four strips
salt and pepper
4 wooden skewers, soaked in water for 30 minutes

Lemon and thyme
¼ teaspoon thyme leaves
1 small garlic clove, crushed
2 tablespoons olive oil
2 teaspoons freshly squeezed lemon juice

Special soy
¼ teaspoon grated fresh root ginger
1 teaspoon dark soy sauce
1 teaspoon rice wine vinegar
½ teaspoon freshly squeezed lemon juice

½ teaspoon tomato purée
½ teaspoon soft light brown sugar
1 tablespoon sunflower oil

Tomato balsamic
3 cherry tomatoes
3 sunblush tomatoes
2 tablespoons olive oil
½ tablespoon balsamic vinegar
½ teaspoon soft light brown sugar
½ teaspoon tomato purée

Marinades not only add flavour but also tenderize chicken. You can marinate strips of uncooked chicken and then freeze them so that they are ready to cook already marinated.

Reheating the chicken isn't recommended.

Sesame chicken fingers

✎ 5 MINUTES, PLUS 1 HOUR
FOR MARINATING

▭ 4–6 MINUTES

◷ 4 PORTIONS

❄ SUITABLE FOR FREEZING

2 chicken breast fillets, cut
    into 2 cm (3/4 in) strips
salt and pepper
200 ml (7 fl oz) buttermilk
1 tablespoon lemon juice
1 teaspoon Worcestershire
    sauce
1 teaspoon soy sauce
1/4 teaspoon paprika
1 garlic clove, peeled and
    sliced
125 g (4 1/2 oz) dried
    breadcrumbs or fresh
    white breadcrumbs
40 g (1 1/2 oz) sesame seeds
a little vegetable oil for
    frying

Season the chicken strips with salt and pepper.
In a bowl, combine the buttermilk, lemon juice,
Worcestershire sauce, soy sauce, paprika and
garlic. Add the chicken strips and toss to coat.
Cover and marinate for at least 1 hour or
overnight.

Drain the chicken well. In a large bowl, toss
the breadcrumbs with the sesame seeds and
some salt and pepper, then roll the chicken in the
crumbs to coat. Heat the oil in a large frying pan
and cook for 2–3 minutes on each side, until
golden and cooked through.

*Sesame seeds are rich in protein and minerals
and are a good source of fatty acids and vitamin E.*

Chicken meatballs in barbecue sauce

🔪 20 MINUTES

🔲 20 MINUTES

🍳 24 MEATBALLS

❄ SUITABLE FOR FREEZING

First, make the barbecue sauce. Heat the oil in a saucepan. Add the onion and garlic and fry for 5 minutes, until soft. Transfer half to a mixing bowl. Add the tomato ketchup, water, soy sauce, brown sugar, Worcestershire sauce and balsamic vinegar to the pan with the remaining onion and garlic. Bring to the boil and simmer for 2 minutes. Add the lemon juice. Mix the cornflour with a little cold water and add to the sauce, then stir until thickened.

To make the meatballs, finely chop the chicken in a food processor, then add to the mixing bowl with the onion and garlic. Whiz the bread to make fine breadcrumbs, then add to the bowl, along with the thyme, egg yolk and apple, and mix together. Shape into 24 balls.

Heat a little oil in a frying pan. Fry the balls until lightly golden. Add to the sauce and simmer for 5–8 minutes, until cooked through.

1 tablespoon olive oil
1 onion (about 140 g/5 oz), peeled and finely chopped
1 garlic clove, crushed
100 ml (3½ fl oz) tomato ketchup
400 ml (14 fl oz) water
1½ tablespoons soy sauce
1 tablespoon brown sugar
2 teaspoons Worcestershire sauce
1 teaspoon balsamic vinegar
1 teaspoon lemon juice
1 tablespoon cornflour

For the meatballs
2 chicken breast fillets
1 slice white bread
2 teaspoons chopped thyme
1 egg yolk
1 apple, peeled, cored and grated
a little oil for frying

Mini chicken sausages

⏱ 10 MINUTES, PLUS 1 HOUR FOR CHILLING

🍳 12 MINUTES

🍽 8 PORTIONS

❄ SUITABLE FOR FREEZING

1 tablespoon olive oil
½ small red onion (30 g/ 1 oz), peeled and chopped
2 tablespoons fresh breadcrumbs, from ½ slice white bread, crusts removed
125 g (4½ oz) minced chicken
½ large eating apple, peeled, cored and grated
1 teaspoon chopped parsley
2 tablespoons grated Parmesan
½ chicken stock cube, dissolved in ½ tablespoon boiling water
1 tablespoon flour
3–4 tablespoons sunflower oil, for frying

Heat the olive oil in a pan and sauté the onion for 5 minutes. Transfer to a food processor with the breadcrumbs, minced chicken, apple, parsley, Parmesan and stock, and whiz to combine.

Take a tablespoonful of the mixture and roll into a sausage shape, then repeat with the remaining mixture. Chill the sausages for 1 hour.

Put the flour on a large plate and coat the sausages. Heat the sunflower oil in a frying pan and fry the sausages for 5–6 minutes on a medium heat, turning frequently until golden.

These little sausages are lovely hot or cold, and just the right size for small fingers.

Satay chicken skewers

Mix the ginger, garlic, lime juice, soy sauce, honey and peanut butter in a medium-size bowl. Add the chicken and toss to coat. Cover and marinate in the fridge for at least 30 minutes, or overnight.

Preheat the grill to High and line a grill pan with aluminium foil. Remove the chicken from the marinade and thread one piece onto each skewer. Lay the skewers on the foil and spoon over any marinade that is left in the bowl. Grill for 3–4 minutes on each side, until the chicken is cooked through.

If making the satay dip, put all the ingredients into a small pan and melt together over a low heat, stirring constantly. Bring to the boil and cook for around 1 minute, until thickened. Remove from the heat and cool to room temperature.

Serve the chicken skewers with the dip. For smaller children, remove the chicken from the skewers and cut into bite-size chunks.

This recipe tastes good cold, too (reheating isn't recommended).

🖊 5 MINUTES, PLUS 30 MINUTES FOR MARINATING

⬛ 10 MINUTES

🍢 4 SKEWERS

❄ SUITABLE FOR FREEZING

½ teaspoon grated fresh root ginger
½ garlic clove, crushed
2 teaspoons freshly squeezed lime juice
2 teaspoons dark soy sauce
2 teaspoons clear honey
4 teaspoons smooth peanut butter
4 chicken mini fillets (about 110 g/4 oz total weight), or 110 g (4 oz) boneless, skinless chicken breast, cut lengthways into 4 strips
4 wooden skewers, soaked in water for 30 minutes

Satay dip (optional)
50 g (2 oz) smooth peanut butter
3 tablespoons coconut milk
2 tablespoons water
2 teaspoons sweet chilli sauce
½ teaspoon dark soy sauce

Chicken, squash and pea risotto

Preheat the oven to 170°C/325°F/Gas 3. Heat 1 tablespoon of oil in an ovenproof saucepan or casserole dish. Add the onion and fry for 3 minutes. Stir in the garlic, then the rice. Add the stock, thyme and squash. Bring to the boil, then cover and transfer to the oven for 15 minutes, adding the peas for the last 5 minutes.

While the risotto is cooking, heat the remaining oil in a small frying pan and fry the chicken until just cooked.

Remove the risotto from the oven. Stir in the chicken, butter and Parmesan. Serve immediately.

🔪 15 MINUTES

▢ 20 MINUTES

◔ 4–5 PORTIONS

❄ SUITABLE FOR FREEZING

2 tablespoons olive oil
1 medium onion (about 140 g/5 oz), peeled and chopped
1 garlic clove, crushed
125 g (4½ oz) risotto rice
450 ml (¾ pint) chicken stock
1 teaspoon chopped thyme
100 g (3½ oz) butternut squash, peeled, deseeded and diced
50 g (2 oz) frozen peas
1 chicken breast fillet, chopped
a knob of butter
40 g (1½ oz) Parmesan cheese, grated

Chicken provides a good source of high-value protein and all the essential amino acids that are so important for growing muscles.

Chicken noodles

/ 7 MINUTES

15 MINUTES

4 PORTIONS

SUITABLE FOR FREEZING

1 medium carrot (about
   100 g/3½ oz), peeled and
   diced
100 g (3½ oz) medium egg
   noodles
2 tablespoons sesame oil
1 medium onion (about 140 g/
   5 oz), peeled and sliced
½ yellow pepper, washed,
   deseeded and diced
1 garlic clove, crushed
1 chicken breast fillet, cut
   into strips
2 teaspoons oyster sauce
2 teaspoons soy sauce
2 teaspoons sweet chilli
   sauce
2 tablespoons drained
   tinned sweetcorn

Bring a saucepan of water to the boil, then
add the carrot and cook for 10 minutes. Add
the noodles to the pan towards the end of the
cooking time – consult the packet instructions
to find out how long the noodles will take to cook.

Meanwhile, heat the oil. Add the onion and
pepper and fry for 3–4 minutes. Add the garlic
and chicken, and fry until the chicken is just
cooked.

Drain the carrots and noodles. Add them to
the frying pan, along with the oyster sauce, soy
sauce, sweet chilli sauce and sweetcorn. Toss
together and serve.

Toasted chicken tortilla

Put the chicken into a bowl. Drizzle over the honey, then season. Heat 1 tablespoon of oil in a small frying pan and fry the chicken for 4–6 minutes, until cooked, then set aside.

Put the spring onions, Cheddar, sweetcorn, basil and mayonnaise into a small bowl. Thinly slice the chicken, then combine with the mixture.

Heat a griddle pan until hot. Put the tortillas in the pan and gently warm through – this will make them easier to roll. Place a tortilla on a work surface, put a quarter of the chicken mixture on one side of the tortilla, then roll up, making sure that the edge is underneath to hold it in place. Repeat with the remaining tortillas.

Brush both sides of each tortilla with a little oil, then fry on both sides until the outside is chargrilled, the filling is warm and the cheese is starting to melt.

/ 3 MINUTES

15–20 MINUTES

8 PORTIONS

SUITABLE FOR FREEZING

180 g (6 oz) chicken breast
  fillet
1 teaspoon runny honey
salt and pepper
2 tablespoons olive oil
3 spring onions, washed
  and finely sliced
25 g (1 oz) Cheddar cheese,
  grated
3 tablespoons drained
  tinned sweetcorn
2 tablespoons roughly
  chopped basil
4 tablespoons mayonnaise
4 tortilla wraps

Chinese chicken and rice

✎ 7 MINUTES

▦ 15 MINUTES

🍴 4 PORTIONS

❄ SUITABLE FOR FREEZING

150 g (5 oz) long grain rice
1 tablespoon olive oil
1 medium onion (about
    140 g/5 oz), peeled and
    chopped
40 g (1 ½ oz) red pepper,
    washed, deseeded and
    diced
4 spring onions, washed
    and sliced
1 chicken breast fillet,
    chopped
1 garlic clove, crushed
1 tablespoon soy sauce
1 tablespoon sweet chilli
    sauce
salt and pepper

Cook the rice according to the packet instructions
and drain.

Meanwhile, heat the olive oil. Add the onion
and sauté for 5 minutes. Add the pepper and fry
for 3 minutes. Add the spring onions, chicken and
garlic. Fry until the chicken is just cooked. Add
the soy sauce, sweet chilli sauce and rice. Toss
together and season well.

*Garlic is good for maintaining a healthy heart
and warding off colds. It has been proven to help
develop resistance to infection, as it contains
allicin, which acts as a natural antibiotic and
antifungal.*

Meat

Annabel's goulash express

Put the steak on a chopping board, cover with clingfilm and beat with a mallet or rolling pin until 3 mm (⅛ in) thick. Cut into thin strips.

Heat the oil in a wok or large frying pan and sear the beef for 3 minutes; it should still be pink inside. Transfer the beef to a plate and set aside.

Return the wok to the heat and add the onion, garlic and red pepper. Sauté for 2 minutes, until soft, then add the paprika and smoked paprika and sauté for a further 3 minutes. Add the tinned tomatoes and tomato purée, stock and sugar, bring to the boil and simmer for 10 minutes. Turn the heat to very low, add the beef to the wok and cook very gently for 5 minutes. Try not to boil the sauce once the beef has been added. Remove from the heat, season to taste and stir in the crème fraîche. Sprinkle over the parsley, if using.

Buttered noodles are a common accompaniment. Cook 200 g (7 oz) tagliatelle according to the packet instructions, drain, and toss with a knob of butter. Divide between 4 plates and spoon over the goulash. Alternatively, you could serve this with rice.

🔪 10 MINUTES

🍳 25 MINUTES

🍴 4 PORTIONS

❄️ SUITABLE FOR FREEZING

350 g (12 oz) sirloin steak, trimmed of fat
1 tablespoon olive oil
1 medium onion (about 140 g/5 oz), peeled and chopped
1 garlic clove, crushed
½ red pepper, washed, deseeded and cut into matchsticks
1 teaspoon paprika
¼ teaspoon smoked paprika
400 g (14 oz) tinned chopped tomatoes
2 tablespoons tomato purée
125 ml (4 fl oz) beef stock
½ teaspoon sugar
salt and pepper
2 tablespoons crème fraîche or soured cream
1 tablespoon chopped parsley (optional)

Beef skewers with balsamic brown-sugar glaze

 10 MINUTES, PLUS 15 MINUTES FOR MARINATING

 10–15 MINUTES

 4 SKEWERS

NOT SUITABLE FOR FREEZING

2 tablespoons balsamic
   vinegar
1½ tablespoons soft light
   brown sugar
1 tablespoon water
150 g (5 oz) fillet or sirloin
   steak, cut into 1 cm (⅓ in)
   cubes
4 wooden skewers, soaked
   in water for 20 minutes

Don't be tempted to marinate the meat for too long – the vinegar is acidic and will break down the meat proteins quickly, which means the meat will turn mushy.

Put the balsamic vinegar, sugar and water in a small saucepan over a medium heat. Bring to the boil, stirring continuously, then lower the heat and simmer for 2–3 minutes, until the mixture has reduced by half and looks syrupy. Pour into a bowl and leave to cool for 5 minutes. Add the beef and toss to coat. Leave to marinate for 10–15 minutes.

Preheat the grill to High and line a grill pan with aluminium foil.

Slide the beef cubes onto the skewers and sit them on the foil-lined grill pan. Spoon over half of the marinade left in the bowl and grill for 3–4 minutes. Turn the skewers, spoon on the remaining marinade, and grill for a further 3–4 minutes, until the beef is cooked through.

Transfer the skewers to a plate and spoon over any juices left on the foil. Cool slightly. For smaller children, it may be best to remove the skewers before serving. Any leftovers will keep, covered, in the fridge for up to 2 days.

Barbecue-style beef

Put the steak on a chopping board, cover with clingfilm and beat with a mallet or rolling pin until it is thin. Slice into strips. Heat 1 tablespoon of the oil in a frying pan and quickly brown the beef on both sides, then set aside.

Heat the remaining oil, add the onion and fry until soft. Add the garlic, then all the remaining ingredients except the cornflour. Bring to the boil. Mix the cornflour with 1 tablespoon of cold water. Add to the sauce and stir until thickened. Return the beef to the pan and simmer for 2 minutes.

🔪 8 MINUTES

🔳 12 MINUTES

🍽 4 PORTIONS

❄ NOT SUITABLE FOR FREEZING

200 g (7 oz) sirloin steak
2 tablespoons olive oil
1 medium onion (about 140 g/5 oz), peeled and finely chopped
1 garlic clove, crushed
250 ml (8 fl oz) beef stock
3 tablespoons tomato ketchup
1 tablespoon soy sauce
2 teaspoons lemon juice
½ teaspoon Worcestershire sauce
2 teaspoons brown sugar
2 teaspoons tomato purée
1 teaspoon cornflour

Red meat is the best source of readily absorbed iron, and should be included in the diet 2 or 3 times a week. The body requires most iron when it's growing fast, so it is especially important to make sure your child gets enough iron between 6 months and 2 years.

Thyme, garlic and lemon lamb chops with couscous

8 MINUTES, PLUS 1 HOUR FOR MARINATING

10–15 MINUTES

2 PORTIONS

NOT SUITABLE FOR FREEZING

4 sprigs fresh thyme
2 teaspoons lemon juice
1 garlic clove, crushed
2 tablespoons olive oil
4 lamb chops

Couscous
100 g (3½ oz) couscous
200 ml (7 fl oz) boiling water
30 g (1 oz) dried apricots, diced
30 g (1 oz) sultanas or raisins
juice of ½ a lemon
1 tablespoon olive oil
1 tablespoon chopped chives
salt and pepper

Pull the leaves from the thyme sprigs and put in a bowl with the lemon juice, garlic and oil. Add the chops and coat in the marinade. Place the bowl in the fridge and leave to marinate for a minimum of 1 hour.

Preheat the grill to High. Transfer the chops to a baking sheet and place in the grill about 20 cm (8 in) away from the heat source. Grill for 10–15 minutes until properly cooked through. Turn them halfway through the cooking time.

Put the couscous into a large bowl and pour over the boiling water. Cover with clingfilm and leave to soak for 10 minutes. Add the remaining ingredients.

Luscious lamb koftas

Heat the oil in a frying pan and sauté one of the onions until softened. Mix together all the kofta ingredients, except the flour and vegetable oil. Transfer to a food processor and chop for a few seconds. Form the mixture into 14 koftas (short, fat sausage shapes), roll in the flour and sauté in the vegetable oil until golden and cooked through.

Cut the pitta breads in half. Spoon a little yoghurt into each pitta pocket, then stuff each one with a lamb kofta, a slice of cucumber and a slice of tomato.

If you prefer, you could replace the pitta pockets with some couscous or rice.

🖊 10 MINUTES

🖻 20 MINUTES

🍴 14 LAMB KOFTAS

❄ SUITABLE FOR FREEZING

1 tablespoon olive oil
2 onions, peeled and chopped
500 g (1 lb 2 oz) minced lamb
80 g (3 oz) fresh breadcrumbs
2 tablespoons chopped coriander
2 tablespoons chopped parsley
1 tablespoon mild curry powder
2 teaspoons ground cumin
1 egg, lightly beaten
1 beef stock cube, crumbled
1 teaspoon sugar
salt and pepper, to season
plain flour, for rolling
vegetable oil, for frying

To serve
7 standard-size pitta breads
Greek yoghurt
14 slices cucumber
14 slices tomato

Sausage and bean hotpot

✏ 10 MINUTES

🔲 30 MINUTES

🍴 4 PORTIONS

❄ SUITABLE FOR FREEZING

4 good-quality sausages
1 tablespoon olive oil
1 medium carrot (about
    100 g/3½ oz), peeled and
    chopped
1 medium onion (about
    140 g/5 oz), peeled and
    chopped
1 garlic clove, crushed
200 g (7 oz) tinned chopped
    tomatoes
200 g (7 oz) baked beans
1 teaspoon tomato purée
1 teaspoon chopped thyme
150 g (5 oz) potatoes, peeled
    and diced
50 g (2 oz) Cheddar cheese,
    grated

Preheat the oven to 200°C/400°F/Gas 6. Put the sausages onto a baking sheet and roast for 20 minutes, until golden and cooked through.

Meanwhile, heat the oil and carrot in a saucepan. Add the onion and fry for 5 minutes. Add the garlic and fry for 1 minute. Add the tinned tomatoes, baked beans, tomato purée and thyme. Cover and simmer for 10 minutes.

Cook the potatoes in boiling water for 5 minutes, until tender.

When the sausages are cooked, cut each one into 6 slices and add to the beans, then spoon the mixture into an ovenproof dish. Drain the potatoes and scatter on top. Sprinkle with the cheese.

Preheat the grill to High, then pop the hotpot under the grill for 5 minutes, until bubbling.

Meatballs in tomato sauce

To make the meatballs, mix all the ingredients together, then shape into 20 balls.

For the sauce, heat the oil in a saucepan. Add the onion and fry until just soft. Stir in the garlic, then add the tinned tomatoes, tomato purée, oregano and sugar. Simmer for 10 minutes, then add the meatballs. Cover with a lid and simmer for 15 minutes, until the meatballs are cooked.

🔪 15 MINUTES

▦ 30 MINUTES

🥧 6 PORTIONS

❄ SUITABLE FOR FREEZING

250 g (9 oz) minced beef
50 g (2 oz) Parmesan cheese, grated
25 g (1 oz) fresh breadcrumbs
1 egg yolk
2 teaspoons chopped thyme
salt and pepper

Tomato sauce
1 tablespoon olive oil
1 medium onion (about 140 g/5 oz), peeled and chopped
2 garlic cloves, crushed
800 g (28 oz) tinned chopped tomatoes
2 tablespoons tomato purée
1 teaspoon dried oregano
a pinch of sugar

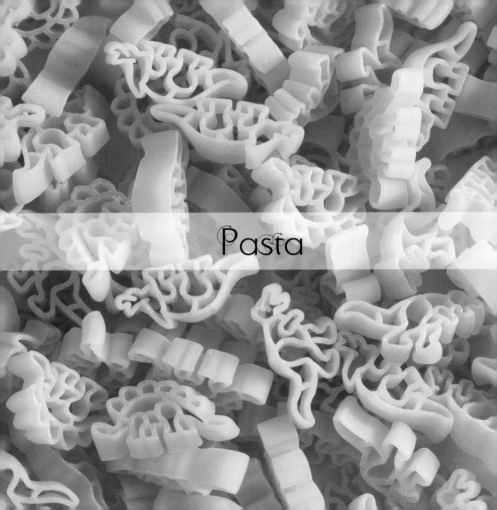

Pasta

Scarlett's spaghettini with chicken, tomatoes and basil

 15 MINUTES

 20 MINUTES

4–5 PORTIONS

SUITABLE FOR FREEZING

Cook the spaghettini according to the packet instructions.

Meanwhile, heat the oil in a fairly large saucepan and sauté the onion for 3 minutes. Add the garlic and chilli flakes and cook for 2 minutes. Add the chicken and cook, stirring, for about 4 minutes, until browned. Add the thyme and parsley and cook for 1 minute. Add the fresh tomatoes and sunblush tomatoes and cook for 2 minutes, then add the chicken stock, frozen peas and basil, and cook for 2 more minutes.

Drain the spaghettini and add to the chicken and tomatoes. Cook, stirring, for 1 minute, then season to taste.

Spaghettini is very thin spaghetti, which can be found in the supermarket. However, you could use spaghetti if you prefer.

250 g (9 oz) spaghettini
2 tablespoons olive oil
1 medium onion (140 g/5 oz),
    peeled and finely chopped
1 large garlic clove, crushed
a good pinch of chilli flakes
2 chicken breasts (about
    250 g/9 oz), cut into strips
1 teaspoon thyme leaves
1 tablespoon chopped flat-
    leaf parsley
4 medium tomatoes
    (285 g/10 oz) skinned,
    deseeded and roughly
    chopped
50 g (2 oz) sunblush
    tomatoes, chopped
350 ml (12 fl oz) chicken
    stock (using 1 stock cube)
75 g (3 oz) frozen peas
1 tablespoon torn basil leaves
salt and pepper

Mighty mac and cheese

- 15 MINUTES
- 15 MINUTES
- 4 PORTIONS
- SUITABLE FOR FREEZING

350 g (12 oz) macaroni
4 medium tomatoes,
    skinned (*see box, below*),
    seeded and chopped
75 g (3 oz) sliced ham,
    shredded (optional)

Cheese sauce
45 g (1½ oz) butter
45 g (1½ oz) flour
450 ml (¾ pint) milk
85 g (3 oz) Gruyère cheese,
    grated
60 g (2 oz) Parmesan
    cheese, grated
150 g (5 oz) mascarpone
    cheese

Topping
40 g (1½ oz) breadcrumbs,
    from 2 medium slices
    white or wholemeal
    bread, crusts removed
20 g (¾ oz) Parmesan
    cheese, grated

Cook the macaroni according to the packet instructions.

Meanwhile, make the cheese sauce. Melt the butter in a saucepan, stir in the flour and cook for 1 minute, stirring constantly. Gradually add the milk and stir over a low heat for 5–6 minutes. Remove from the heat and stir in the Gruyère and Parmesan until melted, then the mascarpone.

Grease an ovenproof dish (about 26 x 17 x 5 cm/10¼ x 6¾ x 2 in) and preheat the grill to High. Drain the pasta and return to the pan. Pour over the cheese sauce and heat through gently. Stir in the tomatoes and ham, if using. Transfer to the prepared dish.

Mix together the topping ingredients and sprinkle on top. Heat under the grill until golden and bubbling.

To remove the skin from a tomato, cut a cross in the base using a sharp knife. Put in a bowl and cover with boiling water. Leave for 1 minute. Drain and rinse in cold water. The skin should peel off easily.

Salmon and broccoli pasta bake

 10 MINUTES

 15 MINUTES

 5 PORTIONS

 SUITABLE FOR FREEZING

150 g (5 oz) fusilli pasta
75 g (3 oz) broccoli florets, washed
30 g (1 oz) butter
1 leek, washed and chopped
3 tablespoons plain flour
450 ml (¾ pint) milk
75 g (3 oz) Parmesan cheese, grated
salt and pepper
150 g (5 oz) salmon fillet, skinned
juice of ½ a lemon
25 g (1 oz) Cheddar cheese, grated
1 tomato, deseeded and chopped

Cook the pasta according to the packet instructions. Add the broccoli 3 minutes before the end of the cooking time, then drain.

While the pasta is cooking, melt the butter in a saucepan, add the leek and stir until softened. Add the flour, then blend in the milk. Stir until thickened and smooth. Add the Parmesan and seasoning.

Put the salmon into a microwave-proof bowl. Pour over the lemon juice, cover with clingfilm and pierce several times. Cook in the microwave on High for 2 minutes.

Flake the salmon and check for any remaining bones, then add the salmon to the sauce, along with the cooking liquid.

Preheat the grill to High. Add the pasta and broccoli to the salmon, mix and transfer to a shallow dish. Sprinkle over the Cheddar and tomato, and put under the grill for 5 minutes until bubbling.

Spaghetti with prawns

Heat the oil in a saucepan. Add the onion and fry for 5 minutes. Add the garlic, then the tomatoes, stock, lemon juice and tomato purée. Simmer for 10 minutes, until reduced but not too thick. Add the prawns 4 minutes before the end of the cooking time to heat through.

Cook the spaghetti according to the packet instructions, drain and add to the sauce. Add the basil. You could serve with some grated Parmesan cheese if you wish.

 5 MINUTES

 20 MINUTES

 4 PORTIONS

 NOT SUITABLE FOR FREEZING

2 tablespoons olive oil
1 medium onion (140 g/
    5 oz), peeled and finely
    chopped
1 garlic clove, crushed
200 g (7 oz) tinned chopped
    tomatoes
200 ml (7 fl oz) fish stock
2 teaspoons lemon juice
1 teaspoon tomato purée
180 g (6 oz) cooked prawns
180 g (6 oz) spaghetti
2 tablespoons chopped basil
Parmesan cheese, grated, to
    serve (optional)

Pasta primavera

⟋ 15 MINUTES

▢ 15 MINUTES

◷ 4–6 PORTIONS

✱ NOT SUITABLE FOR FREEZING

150 g (5 oz) fusilli pasta
2 tablespoons sunflower oil
1 medium onion (140 g/ 5 oz),
  peeled and sliced
150 g (5 oz) butternut squash,
  peeled, deseeded and diced
1 red pepper (100 g/3½ oz),
  washed, deseeded and
  diced
1 medium courgette (100 g/
  3½ oz), washed, topped
  and tailed, and diced
100 g (3½ oz) chestnut
  mushrooms, washed and
  sliced
1 garlic clove, crushed
150 ml (¼ pint) vegetable
  stock
6 tablespoons crème fraîche
60 g (2 oz) Parmesan cheese,
  grated
2 tablespoons chopped basil
a pinch of salt

Cook the pasta following the packet instructions,
then drain.

Heat the oil in a frying pan, then add the
onion and butternut squash, and fry over a low
heat for 5 minutes. Add the pepper, courgette
and mushrooms, and fry for another 3 minutes.
Add the garlic and fry for 1 minute. Add the
vegetable stock to the pan and let it bubble away
until it has reduced by half. Finally, add the
crème fraîche, cheese and basil, then season with
a little salt and toss together with the pasta.

Sweet treats

Mini apricot cheesecakes

Put the biscuits in a freezer bag and crush with a rolling pin to make crumbs. Then mix with the melted butter and cinnamon. Spoon into 6 ramekins, 7.5 cm (3 in) in diameter.

Put the cream and the cream cheese into a bowl and whisk together until smooth and thick. Using an electric hand blender, whiz the apricots until smooth, then add to the cream mixture with the sugar and orange zest.

Spoon on top of the biscuit base and decorate with the apricot slices. Put the cheesecakes in the fridge for 1 hour before serving.

🔪 30 MINUTES, PLUS 1 HOUR FOR CHILLING

🍪 6 RAMEKINS

❄ NOT SUITABLE FOR FREEZING

100 g (3½ oz) digestive biscuits
50 g (2 oz) butter, melted
½ teaspoon ground cinnamon
100 ml (3½ fl oz) whipping cream
100 g (3½ oz) cream cheese
175 g (6 oz) tinned apricots, drained
3 teaspoons caster sugar
¼ teaspoon orange zest
fresh apricots, sliced, to garnish

Apricots are a good source of betacarotene and also contain fibre.

luscious lychee frozen yoghurt

🔪 5 MINUTES, PLUS FREEZING

🍳 6 PORTIONS

❄️ SUITABLE FOR FREEZING

500 ml (17 fl oz) full-fat
 natural yoghurt (500 g/
 1 lb 2 oz pot)
150 ml (¼ pint) single cream
75 g (3 oz) caster sugar
425 g (15 oz) tinned lychees

Mix together the yoghurt, cream and sugar.
Blend the lychees together with 200 ml (7 fl oz)
of the juice from the tin, then combine with the
yoghurt mixture. Freeze and churn the mixture
in an ice-cream maker.

If you don't have an ice-cream maker, pour
the mixture into a shallow container, place in
the freezer for 1 hour, then transfer to a food
processor and whiz until smooth. Freeze for
2 hours, then whiz again and freeze until firm.

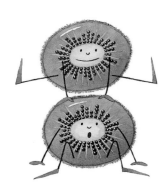

Summer-berry yoghurt ice cream

Put the frozen berries in a small saucepan together with 1 tablespoon of the caster sugar and cook over a gentle heat for a few minutes, until the berries are soft. Purée the fruit and press through a sieve to remove the seeds.

Whip the cream until it forms soft peaks. Mix with the yoghurt, remaining sugar and the fruit purée. Freeze in an ice-cream maker or spoon into a suitable container and put in the freezer.

When half-frozen (about an hour), beat well until smooth. Return to the freezer and stir once or twice during the next hour to make a smooth ice cream.

🔪 5 MINUTES, PLUS FREEZING

▦ 5 MINUTES

🍪 6 PORTIONS

❋ SUITABLE FOR FREEZING

200 g (7 oz) mixed frozen summer fruits (such as strawberries, raspberries, blackberries, blueberries, cherries or redcurrants)
1 tablespoon caster sugar, plus 75 g (3 oz)
200 ml (7 fl oz) double cream
400 ml (14 fl oz) mild natural yoghurt (such as Onken set yoghurt)

Strawberry sundaes

/ 15 MINUTES

▭ 5 MINUTES

◷ 4 SUNDAES

✳ NOT SUITABLE FOR FREEZING

350 g (12 oz) strawberries
a tub of vanilla ice cream

Toffee sauce
150 ml (¼ pint) double cream
30 g (1 oz) butter
30 g (1 oz) dark brown sugar
½ teaspoon vanilla extract

Put 150 g (5 oz) of the strawberries into a jug.
Blend until smooth using a hand blender, to
produce a coulis. Slice the remaining strawberries.

For the toffee sauce, put all the ingredients
into a small saucepan. Stir until the butter has
melted and the sugar has dissolved, then allow
to boil for 1 minute. Leave to cool a little.

Divide half of the sliced strawberries between
4 glasses. Spoon over some of the coulis, then
place a spoonful of ice cream on top. Drizzle over
some of the toffee sauce. Repeat so that you
have 2 layers.

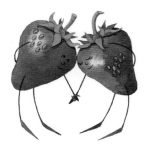

*Strawberries are a great source of vitamin C and
they contain ellagic acid, a phytochemical that
is thought to help in the fight against cancer.*

Frozen berries with hot white-chocolate sauce

To freeze the berries, line a rimmed baking sheet with parchment or greaseproof paper and arrange the berries in a single layer, then put them in the freezer. When they are frozen, transfer to small freezer bags. They will last for 1 month and are also good in smoothies.

Remove the berries from the freezer and divide between 2 bowls. Allow them to defrost slightly at room temperature for around 10 minutes.

Put the chocolate and cream in a microwave-proof jug and heat for 10 seconds. Stir, then repeat, heating and stirring until the chocolate has just melted (it will take 4–5 blasts) and you have a smooth sauce. Alternatively, put the cream and chocolate in a small bowl over a pan of simmering water and stir continuously until the chocolate has just melted.

Pour the hot sauce over the berries straight away and serve immediately.

10 MINUTES, PLUS FREEZING

2 MINUTES

2 PORTIONS

NOT SUITABLE FOR FREEZING

150 g (5 oz) mixed berries (such as blackberries, raspberries, blueberries, strawberries or redcurrants)
55 g (2 oz) white chocolate, chopped into small pieces
60 ml (2 fl oz) double cream

Chocolate fridge cake

5 MINUTES, PLUS 1 HOUR FOR CHILLING

5 MINUTES

12 PORTIONS

NOT SUITABLE FOR FREEZING

150 g (5 oz) milk chocolate
50 g (2 oz) plain chocolate
50 g (2 oz) unsalted butter
200 g (7 oz) digestive biscuits, broken into small pieces
75 g (3 oz) dried apricots, chopped
50 g (2 oz) raisins
50 g (2 oz) pecan nuts, chopped
25 g (1 oz) Rice Krispies
100 g (3½ oz) double cream

Line a 20 cm (8 in) square shallow baking tin with clingfilm, leaving some hanging over the sides.

Put the chocolate and butter in a heatproof bowl and melt over a pan of simmering water, stirring occasionally. Make sure the bottom of the bowl doesn't touch the water.

Mix together the broken biscuits, dried apricots, raisins, pecan nuts and Rice Krispies. Stir the cream into the melted chocolate, then combine with the biscuit mixture. Spoon into the prepared tin and level the surface by pressing down well with a potato masher. Leave to cool in the tin, then place in the fridge to set (this will take 1–2 hours).

To serve, turn out, carefully peel off the clingfilm and cut into 12 squares or triangles.

You can try other combinations of biscuits, fruit and nuts; for example, half digestive and half ginger biscuits, with dried cranberries instead of raisins.

This will keep for up to 2 weeks in the fridge. Well, maybe not ...

Apricot and white-chocolate Rice Krispie squares

Line a 20 cm (8 in) square shallow baking tin with baking paper.

Put the chocolate, butter and golden syrup into a heatproof bowl and melt over simmering water. In a large bowl, mix together the Rice Krispies, porridge oats, dried apricots and pecan nuts. Stir in the melted chocolate mixture.

Spoon the mixture into the prepared tin and level the surface with a potato masher. Place in the fridge to set for a couple of hours, then turn out, peel off the baking paper and cut into 9 squares.

🖊 3 MINUTES, PLUS 1 HOUR FOR CHILLING

⬛ 5 MINUTES

🍽 9 PORTIONS

❄ SUITABLE FOR FREEZING

100 g (3½ oz) white chocolate
75 g (3 oz) unsalted butter
75 g (3 oz) golden syrup
65 g (2½ oz) Rice Krispies
65 g (2½ oz) porridge oats
50 g (2 oz) dried apricots, chopped
30 g (1 oz) pecan nuts, finely chopped

Adding oats for long-lasting energy, nuts for protein and dried apricots for betacarotene gives these Rice Krispie squares a healthy twist.

My favourite ginger biscuits

⬤ 5 MINUTES

⬛ 20 MINUTES

⬤ 6 PORTIONS

✳ SUITABLE FOR FREEZING

65 g (2½ oz) butter, at room
   temperature
50 g (2 oz) soft brown sugar
4 tablespoons golden syrup
1 egg yolk
150 g (5 oz) plain flour, sifted
1 teaspoon ground ginger
½ teaspoon bicarbonate
   of soda

Icing
225 g (8 oz) icing sugar
2–3 tablespoons water
edible silver balls, to
   decorate (optional)

Beat the butter, sugar, syrup and egg yolk with
an electric mixer until the mixture turns pale.
Add the flour, ginger and bicarbonate of soda, and
beat together to form a dough. Wrap in clingfilm
and refrigerate for at least 30 minutes, until firm.

Preheat the oven to 180°C/350°F/Gas 4 and
line two baking sheets with baking paper. Roll
out the dough on a floured surface to about
3 mm (⅛ in) thick.

Cut into shapes using cookie cutters, working
from the outer edges of the dough, cutting the
shapes as close together as possible. Gather
up the trimmings, roll out again and cut more
shapes. Place them on the prepared sheets and
bake for about 8 minutes. Allow to stand, then
transfer to a wire rack to cool completely.

To make the icing, sift the icing sugar into a
bowl and gradually beat in just enough water to
give a smooth icing that is thick enough to pipe.

Cut some greaseproof paper into 15–18 cm
(6–7 in) squares, then cut in half to make triangles.
Roll into cones and fold over the wide end to secure.
Decorate the cookies with the icing and, if you
wish, add edible silver balls.

Meal planner

	Day 1	Day 2	Day 3
Breakfast	**Perfect scrambled eggs** Toast fingers Fruit	**Annabel's granola** Yoghurt Fruit	Cereal **Berry burst**
Lunch	**Sticky salmon** **Easy Chinese fried rice** Fruit	**Barbecue-style beef** Rice, carrots and broccoli **Summer-berry yoghurt ice cream**	**Chicken noodles** Fruit
Dinner	**Sesame chicken fingers** Chips and vegetables Fruit	**Mini fish pie** Fruit	**Carrot and pea risotto** Fruit

This meal planner is intended to be used as a guide.
It's fine to give the same meal more than once in the
same week. Give water or diluted fruit juice with lunch
and dinner.

Day 4	Day 5	Day 6	Day 7
Soft-boiled egg with Italian soldiers Fruit	Cereal Cheese Fruit	**Toasted crumpets with banana and peanut butter** Yoghurt Fruit	Cereal **Ham and cheese muffins** Fruit
Posh fish fingers Broccoli and carrots **Strawberry sundae**	**Thyme, garlic and lemon lamb chops with couscous** Fruit	**Scarlett's spaghettini with chicken, tomatoes and basil** Yoghurt	**Crudités and dips Carrot and sweetcorn fritters** Jelly
Mighty mac and cheese Luscious lychee frozen yoghurt	**Cod in cheesy sauce Mini apricot cheesecake**	**Tortilla Pizza Margherita** Fruit	**Meatballs in tomato sauce** Rice **Luscious lychee frozen yoghurt**

You may wish to give your toddler snacks in between meals.
For some suggestions, see page 7.

Index

About Annabel Karmel

Mother of three, Annabel Karmel MBE is the UK's number one parenting author and expert on devising delicious, nutritious meals for babies, toddlers and children.

Since launching with *The Complete Baby and Toddler Meal Planner* more than two decades ago, Annabel has written 37 books, which have sold over 4 million copies worldwide, covering every stage of a child's development.

With the sole aim of helping parents give their children the very best start in life, Annabel's tried-and-tested recipes have also grown into a successful supermarket food range. From delicious Organic Baby Purées to her best-selling healthy chilled meals, these offer the goodness of a home-cooked meal for those busy days.

Annabel was awarded an MBE in 2006, in the Queen's Birthday Honours, for her outstanding work in child nutrition. She also has menus in some of the largest leisure resorts in Britain and a successful app, *Annabel's Essential Guide to Feeding Your Baby and Toddler*.

For more information and recipes, visit **www.annabelkarmel.com**.

Acknowledgements

Louise Ward and Phil Carroll (Sainsbury's Books), Fiona MacIntyre, Martin Higgins and Cat Dowlett (Ebury), Dave King (photography), Tamsin Weston (props), Kate Bliman and Maud Eden (food stylists), Lucinda McCord (recipe testing), Nick Eddison and Katie Golsby (Eddison Sadd), and Sarah Smith (PR).

annabel karmel

Other titles in the series are:

ANNABEL KARMEL'S FAVOURITES

First foods

Recipes and advice to help you wean your baby

Suitable from four months

ANNABEL KARMEL'S FAVOURITES

Exploring new tastes

Introduce your baby to new flavours and textures

Suitable from six to nine months

ANNABEL KARMEL'S FAVOURITES

Growing independence

Healthy home-made recipes to encourage self-feeding

Suitable from nine to twelve months

ANNABEL KARMEL'S FAVOURITES

Lunchboxes

Quick, easy and healthy ideas to make lunchtime fun

50 *healthy recipes*

ANNABEL KARMEL'S FAVOURITES

Tasty food for fussy kids

Great recipes to tempt your picky eater

50 *healthy recipes*

ANNABEL KARMEL'S FAVOURITES

Family meals

Quick and easy recipes to keep meal times fresh

50 *healthy recipes*

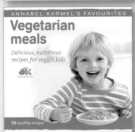

ANNABEL KARMEL'S FAVOURITES

Vegetarian meals

Delicious, nutritious recipes for veggie kids

50 *healthy recipes*

ANNABEL KARMEL'S FAVOURITES

Party food

Quick, quirky and fun ideas for your child's celebration

50 *healthy recipes*

ANNABEL KARMEL'S FAVOURITES

Kids in the Kitchen

Creative recipe ideas to make and bake together

50 *healthy recipes*